THE LORD'S TABLE

Stephen Kaung

ISBN: 978-1-942521-24-2

Available from:

Christian Testimony Ministry
4424 Huguenot Road
Richmond, Virginia 23235

www.christiantestimonyministry.com

Printed in USA

CONTENTS

THE LORD'S TABLE

Acts 2:42—And they persevered in the teaching and fellowship of the apostles, in breaking of bread and prayers.

I Corinthians 10:16-22—The cup of blessing which we bless, is it not the communion of the blood of the Christ? The bread which we break, is it not the communion of the body of the Christ? Because we, being many, are one loaf, one body; for we all partake of that one loaf. See Israel according to flesh: are not they who eat the sacrifices in communion with the altar? What then do I say? that what is sacrificed to an idol is anything, or that an idol is anything? But that what the nations sacrifice they sacrifice to demons, and not to God. Now I do not wish you to be in communion with demons. Ye cannot drink the Lord's cup, and the cup of demons: ye cannot partake of the Lord's table, and of the table of demons. Do we provoke the Lord to jealousy? are we stronger that he?

I Corinthians 11:23-32—For I received from the Lord, that which I also delivered to you, that the Lord Jesus, in the night in which he was delivered up, took break, and having given thanks broke it, and said, This is my body, which is for you: this do in remembrance of me. In like manner also the cup, after having supped, saying, This cup is the new covenant in my blood: this do, as often as ye shall drink it, in remembrance of me. For as often as ye shall eat this bread, and drink the cup, ye announce the death of the Lord, until he come. So that whosoever shall eat the bread, or drink the cup of the Lord, unworthily, shall be guilty in respect of the body and of the blood of the Lord. But let a man prove himself, and thus eat of the bread, and drink of the cup. For the eater and drinker eats and drinks judgment to himself, not distinguishing the body. On this account many among you are weak and infirm, and a good many are fallen asleep. But if we judged ourselves, so were we not judged. But being judged, we are disciplined of the Lord, that we may not be condemned with the world.

Shall we pray:

Dear heavenly Father, what a joy and privilege that Thou hast invited us to the table of the Lord. We do praise and thank Thee that in ourselves we are never worthy, but Thou hast made us worthy that we may come and sup with Thee and commune with Thee to praise and worship Thee. So, Lord, as we continue in Thy presence we do pray that Thou wilt breathe upon Thy word and make it living to each of our hearts that whenever we come together to remember Thee, it would be real and living and with eternal value. And to Thee be all the glory. In the name of the Lord Jesus. Amen.

The Holy Spirit uses one sentence to sum up the life and testimony of the early church. That sentence is in Acts 2:42. All those who believed in the Lord lived in the breaking of bread and in prayers, in the teaching and fellowship of the apostles. Not only the twelve apostles, not only the hundred and twenty who waited in the upper room for ten days before Pentecost, but also the three thousand who came to the Lord on that day of Pentecost persevered, continued, lived constantly in the teaching and fellowship of the apostles, in breaking of bread and prayers. This was how the early church lived, and this was their testimony to the world.

THE TEACHING AND FELLOWSHIP OF THE APOSTLES

Notice here, it does not say the *teachings* of the apostles. It says the "teaching" of the apostles. There were twelve apostles at that time, but they did not have twelve different teachings, although each of them was different. Peter was different from John, and James was different from Andrew. And as we read the New Testament, we may even find they have different emphases. It is very clear if you read something written by John. Even though his name may not appear, you know it is John. And if you try to read something of Peter, even though you may not notice his name, you know it is Peter. In other words, all these apostles, not only the twelve apostles, but all the apostles, such as Paul and others, each has his emphasis of teaching, and yet there is only one teaching, not many teachings. Peter does not have his own teaching; John does not have his own teaching; Paul does not have his own teaching; James does not have his own teaching. They all taught what the Lord Jesus had taught them. In other words, the teaching of the apostles is singular in number. The teaching of the apostles is none other than the teaching of the Lord. So, if you continue on in Acts 13:12 you find, "the teaching of the Lord." The proconsul in Paphos was amazed at the teaching of the Lord, even though it was Paul who was teaching it.

All those in the early church who believed in the Lord Jesus continued in the teaching of the Lord and they continued in the fellowship of the apostles. Again, it is not *fellowships.* It is singular: "fellowship." Even though there were a number of apostles, their fellowship is one because it is the fellowship of God's Son, Jesus Christ. Paul does not have his own fellowship; John does not have his own fellowship; Peter does not have his own fellowship. But you find they are all in that one fellowship, the fellowship of God's Son, Jesus Christ.

So, in I Corinthians 1:9, Paul wrote: "God is faithful, by whom ye have been called into the fellowship of his Son Jesus Christ our Lord." We are all being called into the fellowship of God's Son, Jesus Christ. The fellowship of the apostles is none other than the fellowship of God's Son, Jesus Christ.

In I John 1:3, John says, "That which we have seen and heard we report to you, that ye also may have fellowship with us; and our fellowship is indeed with the Father, and with his Son Jesus Christ." This was the way all the believers in the early church lived. That was the way they continued on together in the teaching and the fellowship of the apostles; that is, in the teaching of the Lord, in the fellowship of God's Son, Jesus Christ. This was the way the early church taught and lived. And this is the way that we should teach; this is the way that we should live.

PUBLIC EXPRESSION

Teaching is concerned with truth. Fellowship is related to life. It is well-balanced. On the one hand, it is the teaching of the truth; on the other hand, it is the fellowship of life, of love. It is well-balanced, not one-sided. This was the way the early church lived. And as they continued in the teaching and fellowship of the apostles, you find public expression of their perseverance in the teaching and fellowship of the apostles.

The public expression of it is the breaking of bread and prayer. Sometimes we do not think too much about the breaking of bread, or the Lord's table, or the Lord's supper. Sometimes we neglect this matter of prayers. The prayers here do not refer to our personal private prayer. We do know the importance of our private prayer. The prayer here is corporate prayer. The church comes together to pray, just like the church comes together to remember the Lord in the breaking of bread.

Today in Christianity people do not think too much of this matter of the breaking of bread. There are places where they do not break the bread. For instance, the Friends, the Quakers, do not break the bread at all. They think it is just symbolic, just an outward form, and they are delivered from these outward things because they have entered into the spirit. In some places, you find there will be the communion once a month, in other places, maybe only twice a year at Easter and Christmas. People do not think much about the breaking of bread. But in the early church, this was *the* expression of their continuance in the teaching and fellowship of the apostles.

Likewise in Christianity today, people do not think too much about praying together. In some places, there is no corporate prayer. They come on Sunday and spend an hour; that is enough. They do not care about coming to pray together. In other places, maybe there is a prayer meeting, but only a few, maybe three or five will be there. God's people do not put much emphasis on this matter of corporate prayer. People do not come together to pray. They think it is just too much. But in the early church, this was their life, their testimony. These two things—the breaking of bread and prayers—were the public life and testimony of the early church. Today we will concentrate on this matter of the breaking of bread.

Sometimes, we think the breaking of bread is just a ritual, or just a tradition; or, we may do it so often that we take it as something very common. We have to remember that this breaking of bread is instituted by none other than our Lord Jesus Himself. On the night of His betrayal, He gathered His disciples, His own family in the upper room with Him to eat that Passover feast. Towards the end of that feast, He took the bread, He blessed it and gave to His disciples and said, "Take, eat; this is My body." Afterward, He took the cup, gave thanks, gave it to the disciples and said, "This is My blood of the new covenant. Drink ye all of it." It is the blood of the new covenant shed for the remission of sins.

So on that night, our Lord Jesus gave to His church this breaking of bread to remember Him. And since that day, the church has been doing this very thing. Now, this was not only done in Jerusalem, in Judea, or Samaria, but this was continually done by the Gentile churches. God raised up Paul, and through his ministry raised up many churches among the Gentiles. They were doing the very same thing. It was not only done by the Jewish church but by the Gentile church too, because in Christ there is neither Jew nor Gentile.

Now of course, Paul had not seen the Lord. He was not a disciple of the Lord when the Lord was on earth. So he had not heard what the Lord had said about this breaking of bread, yet in I Corinthians 11, he said, "What I have received of the Lord, that I have delivered unto you." Evidently Paul received a revelation. The risen Lord told Paul that wherever he went, wherever the church is established, they should have the breaking of bread as a public testimony, as their public life.

Before His death, in view of Calvary, the Lord gave us this breaking of bread, but even after He was ascended and was seated at the right hand of the Father, He still commanded us to do this in remembrance of Him. How important it is to the

Lord! Again and again, He reminded His people: "Do this in remembrance of Me."

Why does our Lord remind us so much to do this? Is He afraid that we may forget Him? How can we forget Him who died for us, who loved us so much, who gave Himself for us? Dear brothers and sisters, He knows our frailty. But more than that, the reason it is as if the Lord is insisting that His own do this is because He loves us so much that He wants us to remember Him. He loves us so much that He does not want us to depart from our first love. The relationship between the Lord and us is a love relationship. It is not a mental thing; it is not a physical matter. It is a love relationship. He loves us and gave Himself for us. He loved us and He loved us to the uttermost. He completely laid down His life for His own. Because He loves us so much, He wants us to love Him too. The one thing that He desires of His people is first love. First love means first in time and first in quality. It means that we love Him as He has loved us. The only way He can keep us in this first love is to constantly put His love before our eyes.

How easily we are enticed! How easy it is for us to look at this or that and our hearts be led away to many things. The Lord said, "Do this in remembrance of Me." This is the way. This is His love for us. He wants to keep His love ever before our eyes that we may not depart from that first love towards Him. We thank the Lord He asks us to remember Him. It is not cumbersome, it is for our benefit, for our good; and this is His command. Because this is His command, we ought to do it.

There is something the enemy hates very much. The enemy hates for God's people to come together to break bread. Have you ever thought of that? The enemy hates to see God's people come together to pray. We have heard that the devil trembles when a saint is on his knees. Now, if God's people come together to pray, it shakes hell. That is why he tries every means to prevent God's people from coming together to pray. The same is true with the breaking of bread. If you think of what he has done to God's people today concerning this matter of the breaking of bread, you can see how clever he is in his device. For instance, there are some people who really think very highly of this breaking of bread, of this communion, of this Lord's supper. They do see that this is the center of the life of the church and they do make it the center of church life, of church service. But see how clever the devil is? He knows he is not able to take it away, so he tries to change its character and he makes the breaking of bread a mass.

What is a mass? A mass is a re-enactment of crucifixion. Through the blessing of the priest, actually that bread is transformed into the physical body of the Lord Jesus. So people are eating the very flesh of the Lord Jesus when they take the bread. Through the blessing of the priest, the wine is physically transformed into the blood of the Lord Jesus. So you are blood drinkers—transubstantiation. That is what a large group of so-called believers in Christendom believe. They believe in transubstantiation: that the wine is transformed into the blood and you drink it; that the bread is transformed into the physical body of the Lord Jesus and you eat it. In other words, he makes everything physical instead of that spiritual reality.

How many times must our Lord Jesus be crucified? Every time they celebrate a mass, our Christ is supposed to be crucified once over. He has been crucified numberless times during these twenty centuries. Isn't that a blasphemy? In Hebrews 10, it says once and for all our Lord Jesus offered Himself as a sacrifice, and He has completed that eternal redemption. He does not need to die anymore—once; that is enough. He is now alive and He is living forevermore. We are worshiping a living Christ. In Hebrews 6, it says if you recrucify the Lord Jesus, you make a public disgrace of Him. So here you see how wise the enemy is. He tries to turn it into something else, something unscriptural, something other than what the Lord means it to be. And because it has become so mystical, it has lost its meaning. People are taking it as something mysterious.

On the other hand, you find many people, the so-called Protestants, who see the device of the enemy in trying to turn the breaking of bread into a mass. So they say, "No, no this is just symbolic." When the Lord Jesus says, "This is My body," they say, "No, He means, 'This represents My body; it is not really My body.'" When He says, "This is My blood," they say, "Of course, this is not His blood, it just represents His blood." So when they do it, it is just a symbolic thing. When you reduce it into the symbolic, you dismiss it into the secondary.

In the Protestant church, the primary thing in the service is the preaching of the Word, the ministry of the Word, the sermon. The sermon is the center of worship. Now actually, the sermon is for the benefit of God's people. It cannot be considered as the center of worship because worship should be centered on the Lord and not on the Lord's people. Here we are being deceived by the enemy to become so self-centered that even when we come to worship God, it is for our benefit only. So in the Protestant churches, the sermon or the ministry of the Word takes the first place. They dismiss the breaking of bread to a secondary position. In some places it is not even celebrated, or in other places it is only done once in a while. They even say, "If you do it too often, it will become very common." Why? because if it is symbolic, of course it will. So you can see how clever the enemy is. He tries to take away from God's people that public expression of their life and testimony of the Lord.

THE BREAD AND THE CUP

What is the bread? What is the cup? On that night our Lord Jesus took up the loaf and said, "This is My body." He did not say, "This represents My body." He said, "This is My body." When He took up the cup, He said, "This is My blood." He did not say, "This represents My blood." When our Lord was giving it to us, in His mind there was neither transubstantiation nor representation. It is neither mysterious nor symbolic. It is a spiritual reality. We need to see that there is a spiritual reality here. When the Lord says, "This is My body and this is My blood," we need to go beyond the physical and into the spiritual because only that which is spiritual is real and eternal.

The blood of our Lord Jesus was shed on the cross. But even if you had been there on that day, and had gone to the bottom of the cross and drunk some blood from it, would your sins be forgiven? No. Remember, it is not that physical blood, it is what that blood means. It is that blood that redeems us, that substitutes for us, that pays the price before God. You have to see it is the meaning of the blood, the value of the blood, the eternal efficacy of the blood that is *the* reality. It is not just the physical blood. The physical blood is shed for that spiritual eternal reality. So remember this.

As we take the bread, it is still the bread we are eating. We are not eating the physical body of Christ. Then we would be cannibals. You are eating just bread, but when you are eating it, in your eyes of faith, you see the reality of the body of Christ—how that body was broken for your sake that He may join you to Him and us to one another.

When you drink the cup, it is the wine, it is the fruit of the vine. You are not drinking blood. As a matter of fact, in the early days, in the Noahic covenant, after God covenanted with Noah and his sons and the world and the creatures, God said, "You cannot drink blood because life is in the blood." That Noahic covenant is still effective, valid today because the world is still living under the Noahic covenant. There are still winter and summer, cold and heat, harvest and planting. That is the Noahic covenant.

That is why in Acts 15 you find that, although the Gentile believers did not need to keep Moses' law—they did not need to be circumcised—yet they should not drink blood because they are still human beings, still under the Noahic covenant. We are not allowed to drink blood. What we drink is really the fruit of the vine. But with the eyes of faith, we see in that fruit the blood of our Lord Jesus. "This is My blood," the Lord said, "for the remission of your sins." To us, it is the spiritual reality. It is neither symbolic— representative, nor is it transubstantial— mysterious. It is spiritual. It is real.

When we come together to remember the Lord, outwardly we are touching the bread, the cup; but remember, if we just touch it outwardly then this is a ritual, a form, a ceremony. It has lost its meaning. But as we come together and break the bread and as we drink the cup and in our spirit we do see the body of our Lord Jesus broken for us, we do see the blood of our Lord

Jesus shed for us, oh how real it is! You touch reality; you touch God. This is how important it is. Do not make it common. See how important it is that we come again and again to remember the Lord in this way that our love may be renewed.

Do we touch the reality as we come to break the bread and drink the cup? Has it become common to us because we do it so often? How can it be a spiritual reality unless there is revelation, unless God, by His Spirit, opens our spirit's eyes? We need God by His Spirit to open the eyes of our spirit that we see the Lord. Each time we gather to remember the Lord, we need to ask the Lord to give us a fresh revelation, to open our spirit's eyes to see the Lord Himself, to see how He loves us, how He shed His blood for us, how He laid down His life for us. We need to see it in our spirit. Then, with faith we come and partake of it. It is meaningful and it is real and what a blessing it is! You come to the Lord's table and go away without being blessed. How can it be? You come to the Lord's table without seeing the Lord, without feeling a touch of His love, without being stirred in your heart, without your love toward Him being renewed. How can it be? The only reason we can do it in that fashion is because our spirit is dull, we just do it in a formal way without seeing the Lord in our spirit.

The Lord wants to use this as a means for us to see Him. "Remember Me." When you see Him, you will come by faith. You will take this by faith. It will only be blessing and no curse.

This is the reason the apostle Paul explains to us what the breaking of bread really means. In I Corinthians 10, he says, "The cup of blessing which we bless, is it not the communion of the blood of the Christ? The bread which we break, is it not the communion of the body of the Christ? Because we, being many, are one loaf, one body; for we all partake of that one loaf." This breaking of bread is a communion. It is a communion of the blood of the Christ.

WHAT IS COMMUNION?

Communion is to share something in common, to participate, to take part. When the Lord's people come together around the table and drink the cup and break the bread, this is a communion, a fellowship. We are in communion with the blood of the Lord Jesus. In our spirit we are sharing in common, having a fresh sense of the efficacy, of the preciousness, of the power of His blood. Every time we come to drink the cup, it is as if we refresh our memory of the forgiveness of our sins. Thank God, though our sins be as scarlet, they are now as white as snow. Every time we drink the cup, we thank the Lord for the preciousness of His blood. His blood continuously cleanses us from all our sins that we may stand before God with holy boldness. What a communion that is! Every time we drink the cup, once again we feel the power of that precious blood—the blood that paid for our crime before God, the blood that stills our conscience, the blood that shuts the mouth of the accuser. Once again we experience the blessing of the blood.

This cup is the cup of blessing. In the Garden of Gethsemane, our Lord Jesus drank the cup of curse for us all. He drank every drop of it and He left with us the cup of blessing. We bless the cup of blessing, so it is a communion with the Lord.

COMMUNION OF THE SAINTS

We not only have communion with the blood and the body of our Lord, a communion in our spirit when we are breaking the bread and drinking the cup. We see His beauty; once again we pour forth our fragrance and our thanks toward Him. But, in I Corinthians 10, communion has another emphasis: it is communion in the blood of the Christ, communion in the body of the Christ. It is a communion of the saints. Not only are we in communion with our Christ, we are in communion with our brothers and sisters because we share the same, in spite of all our differences. The differences will remain, and yet there is something we have in common: the blood of the Lord, the body of the Lord. We have the Lord in common. As we are drinking the cup and breaking the bread, it shows that we are in communion with all the brothers and sisters. Though we are many, yet we are one. It is only one loaf, one body.

How blessed it is! It is a fellowship of the saints. That is a public expression of the fellowship of the apostles. We express that we do have fellowship with all God's people, the body of Christ, and what a body that is!

COMMUNION IS INCLUSIVE

Communion, if it is communion, it is all inclusive on the one hand and all exclusive on the other. We can commune only with that which we share in common. If we do not have in common, then there is no communion. As we commune here at the Lord's table, we commune with all the believers throughout the whole world. It cannot be exclusive. Even though there are only few here, this loaf represents the whole body of Christ. We are not just breaking bread with a few, we are breaking bread with all God's people all over the world. This is the body. We are having communion with all of our brothers and sisters, known and unknown to us. One thing we are sure of: we belong to the same body. We have no grudge, no ax to grind, no controversy, no unforgiveness, no bitterness towards any of our brothers and sisters. We embrace them in our hearts. As we come to the Lord's table, it enlarges our hearts. Naturally, we are small, but God wants us to enlarge our hearts. He expands our hearts when we come to the table that we will embrace all of our brothers and sisters all over the world. Thank God we are one!

COMMUNION IS EXCLUSIVE

On the other hand, because this is a communion, this is a fellowship, therefore, it has to be exclusive, that is to say, it has to be separated from the world. The Lord's table separates us from the world. We cannot drink the cup of the demons and come drink the cup of the Lord. We cannot partake of the table of the Lord and then partake of the table of demons. There is no communion, there is no fellowship. In II Corinthians 6, it says that we should not be unequally yoked because there is no fellowship between light and darkness.

As we come to remember the Lord, how we need to be separated from the world. Does the world still have a hold upon us? Are we still trying to serve two masters? This should be settled. The Lord has separated us. He has sanctified us by the Word. Therefore, we need to be separated from the world. Each time we come to remember the Lord, it is a public testimony that we do not belong to the world. That is the reason the world hates us, because we do not belong. We belong to the Lord and we belong to His family. Thank God for that!

So whenever we come together, it is an expression of a oneness in Christ. In the prayer of our Lord Jesus, how He longs that we may be one as He and the Father are one that the world may believe that God hath sent Him. This is it. The breaking of bread is the public testimony to the world that we who believe in the Lord Jesus are one that the world may believe. What a testimony that is! This is the breaking of the bread.

What is the Lord's supper? What does it mean? Paul continues on in I Corinthians 11: On the night the Lord Jesus was betrayed, He took the bread, broke it, blessed it and said, "This is My body; do this in remembrance of Me." And again He took the cup, blessed it and gave it to the disciples and said, "Drink ye all of it, do this in remembrance of Me." The breaking of bread is a remembrance of the Lord. We remember Him.

Remembering is recalling, looking back to two thousand years ago. We remember that He, who loved us so much, was crucified there. Was it two thousand years ago? No, because when we remember Him, the Holy Spirit brings that scene of Calvary to us today. It is as if He died for us today. It is real, it is present, it is living. And it is in that remembrance, through the power of the Holy Spirit, that He brings Christ to us at this very moment, and it ought to refresh our love towards Him. That is the reason He wants us to remember Him, that our love may once again be refreshed, that we may love Him with all our hearts, with all our minds, with all our soul and with all our strength. The Lord Jesus said as long as you drink the cup and break the bread, you announce, show forth the death of the Lord.

The Lord's table is not only a remembrance, it is an announcement. To put it another way, it is an exhibition. What is the church doing? What has the church been doing throughout the centuries? The church is exhibiting the death of the Lord. When people are celebrating the birth of Christ these days, we are exhibiting the death of the Lord because He came to die. It is the death of the Lord that we exhibit because it is death to all deaths. It is by His death He destroyed the one who had the power of death. It is by death that He now holds the keys to death and Hades. It is through that death He brings in life and resurrection life. This is the most glorious death in the whole universe. People like to hide death, so you bury the dead because it is a shame. But thank God, here is a death that is our glory. We love to exhibit that death. We love to announce to the whole world that Christ has died. Because He has died, there is hope. This is our testimony. This is our exhibition. This is our declaration to the world, not only to the seen world, but to the unseen world. You know, it is in that death Satan trembles, because Satan was defeated, is defeated, forever.

Why do we call it an exhibition? How do we exhibit it? As we gather around the table, we find the bread on one side, the cup with the fruit of the vine on the other. When the blood is outside of the body, that speaks of death. All the blood of our Lord Jesus was drained. He was not only scourged badly and blood came forth, not only crowned with a thorny crown and blood came forth, not only was He crucified and blood came forth from His wounds, but even at the very last, when the soldier thrust that spear into His side, out of His broken heart came forth blood and water. He has died. He is the first and the last. He is the living one, but He has become dead and He is now alive and lives forevermore. Brothers and sisters, this is our exhibition. That is why the bread and wine are in separate places. That is why we drink it separately. It represents the death of our Lord Jesus. We will exhibit that death until He comes. It gives us blessed hope. It tells us that one day He is coming back. He is coming back to take us to Himself.

When we come to the Lord's table and we are in touch with Him once again, with our lover, we cannot help but cry out, "Come, Lord Jesus." We have not seen Him but we love Him and we desire that we see Him face to face. Oh, how we hope when we come to break the bread together that this will be the last time we do it here! The next time will be in that glorious day when our Lord Jesus will drink anew with us, and it is the day of His wedding at that marriage feast that He will drink again with us. How we look forward to that day!. It gives us hope when we come to the Lord's table. The world has no hope, but we have hope, and our blessed hope is that our Lord is coming soon.

This is what the breaking of bread means. If we do see what the breaking of bread means, and if we really come in our spirit by faith, then brothers and sisters, we will see what a blessing this is. Because this is real, therefore the apostle Paul says, when you come to break the bread and drink the cup, do not come in an unworthy manner lest you drink your own sin. What does it mean? On the one hand, nobody is worthy. Who is worthy to come to the table of the Lord? We are like that prodigal son. We have wasted away all the grace of God. We have gone to a far country. We are reduced to hunger. We are reduced to do that dirty work and it does not satisfy us. We are not worthy to come back. We are not worthy to sit at His table; but, it is the Father's love, it is the redemption of our Lord Jesus, it is the wooing of the Holy Spirit that makes us worthy to come to the table of the Lord. He has made us worthy. Since He has made us worthy, can we come in an unworthy manner? No. He has made us worthy, therefore, we have to come in a worthy manner.

Now, what does that mean? Paul said when you come, prove yourself first, examine yourself. Do not come casually. Do not come as if it is common. Do not come because it is routine, it is a habit, it is a tradition. Do not come in that way. When you come, prepare yourself. When you come, prove yourself if you are coming in faith. Examine yourself. During the week have you had a controversy with the Lord? Have you been disobedient to the Lord? Do you have sins that have not been confessed and forgiven? We need to examine ourselves before we come that there is nothing between us and the Lord because what we are doing is a real thing. You are not just touching something physical, you are touching something spiritual. Because of this, you need to be prepared for it and also examine yourself to see if you have any controversy with your brothers and sisters, if you hate any brother or sister. Is there any bitterness in your heart, unforgiveness in your heart? Even though some brother may have offended you badly, have you forgiven him? If there is anything between you and any brother and sister in the whole world, let it be confessed and put under the precious blood of Jesus so that you can come and worship Him in a worthy manner.

When we come together, we need to examine ourselves, and we need to distinguish the body. What does it mean by distinguishing the body? It simply means when you come you need to see that this is the body. It is not exclusive, it is not just a few, but we are in fellowship with the whole body of Christ. And if we come in this way, we will not be judged.

Sometimes, there is a question when we come to drink the cup and break the bread whether it will bring some sickness to us. There is such a fear among God's people. Now, remembering the Lord is a most blessed thing and yet we do need to fear, but fear not in that sense, but in another sense. The fear is lest we take it unworthily. We do not need to fear other things because this is the cup of blessing which we bless. But we do need to fear lest we do it unworthily. In the church in Corinth, because they did it unworthily, some got sick, some even died.

When you touch spiritual reality, it is so real, it cannot be more real. On the one hand, there will be serious consequences; but on the other hand, there will be abundant blessing. Nothing blesses our heart or does us more good than being at the Lord's table. Dear brothers and sisters, you are the Lord's, the Lord has invited you to His table, do not purposefully absent yourself from it.

The Lord used a parable. The king had a wedding feast for his son. He invited guests but these guests neglected the invitation. They looked down upon the king and his son. They would not come. Now, do not do that. Sometimes, we do not come to the Lord's table for a very small reason, or no reason at all. There is no excuse. We need to come to the Lord's table. He has invited us.

In the early church, in Acts 2, they broke bread daily from house to house. Daily they met in the temple for the Word of God, the teaching of the apostles, and daily they broke bread from house to house for the fellowship of the apostles. They were in first love. Later on, it became the way of the church to break bread on the first day of the week, that is the Lord's day. In Acts 20, the people in Troas came together on the first day of the week to break bread. Even though they did come together to hear Paul, it was to break bread. Unfortunately, Paul spoke too long and a boy fell down. The important thing was the breaking of bread. They did not come to hear Paul, they came to break bread.

This is why we break bread every Lord's Day. This is the first thing. This is the center. This is the center of our worship to the Lord. This is *the* thing. The others are secondary. I encourage brothers and sisters, do not miss the breaking of bread. Make it a first thing in your life. Oh, what benefit, what blessing will come upon you!

Shall we pray:

Dear heavenly Father, we do praise and thank Thee, we who were unworthy, yet Thou hast made us worthy to come to Thy table to sup with Thee. Oh, how we praise and thank Thee for it. And we do pray that on the one hand Thou will encourage us that we will not look down upon Thy table, but we will gladly come to Thy table. On the other hand, we pray that we may come in a worthy manner. Lord, we do ask Thee that each time we touch the bread and the cup, we may touch Thee and Thou would touch us once again that the love between Thee and us would continually be renewed day to day until we see Thee face to face. We ask in the name of our Lord Jesus. Amen.

Books by Christian Testimony Ministry

SPEAKER	TITLE
DANA CONGDON	MARRIAGE, SINGLENESS, AND THE WILL OF GOD
	RECOVERY & RESTORATION
	THE HOLY SPIRIT
	HEBREWS
A.J. FLACK	TENT OF HIS SPLENDOUR
	ACTS
STEPHEN KAUNG	BE YE THEREFORE PERFECT
	CALLED OUT UNTO CHRIST
	CALLED TO THE FELLOWSHIP OF GOD'S SON
	DIVINE LIFE AND ORDER
	FOR ME TO LIVE IS CHRIST
	GLORIOUS LIBERTY OF THE CHILDREN OF GOD
	GOD'S PURPOSE FOR THE FAMILY
	I WILL BUILD MY CHURCH
	MEDITATIONS ON THE KINGDOM
	RECOVERY
	SPIRITUAL EXERCISE
	SPIRITUAL LIFE (II CORINTHIANS SERIES)
	TEACH US TO PRAY
	THE CROSS
	THE FULNESS OF CHRIST—IN THE BOOK OF REVELATION
	THE HEADSHIP OF CHRIST
	THE KINGDOM AND THE CHURCH
	THE KINGDOM OF GOD
	THE LAST CALL TO THE CHURCHES, THE CALL TO OVERCOME
	THE LIFE OF OUR LORD JESUS
	THE LIFE OF THE CHURCH, THE BODY OF CHRIST
	THE LORD'S TABLE
	TWO GUIDEPOSTS FOR INHERITING THE KINGDOM
	VISION OF CHRIST (REVELATION)
	WHO ARE WE?
	WORSHIP
	WHY DO WE SO GATHER?

LANCE LAMBERT	CALLED UNTO HIS ETERNAL GLORY
	GOD'S ETERNAL PURPOSE
	IN THE DAY OF THY POWER
	JACOB I HAVE LOVED
	LIVING FAITH
	LESSONS FROM THE LIFE OF MOSES
	LOVE DIVINE
	MY HOUSE SHALL BE A HOUSE OF PRAYER
	PREPARATION FOR THE COMING OF THE LORD
	REIGNING WITH CHRIST
	SPIRITUAL CHARACTER
	THE GOSPEL OF THE KINGDOM
	THE IMPORTANCE OF COVERING
	THE LAST DAYS AND GOD'S PRIORITIES
	THE PRIZE
	THE SUPREMACY OF JESUS CHRIST
	THINE IS THE POWER!
	THOU ART MINE
T. AUSTIN-SPARKS	THE LORD'S TESTIMONY AND THE WORLD NEED

HARVEY CEDARS CONFERENCE

STEPHEN KAUNG	HEAVENLY VISION
	SPIRITUAL RESPONSIBILITY
CONGDON, HILE, KAUNG	SPIRITUAL MINISTRY
	SPIRITUAL AUTHORITY
	SPIRITUAL HOUSE
	SPIRITUAL SUBMISSION
STEPHEN KAUNG	SPIRITUAL KNOWLEDGE
	SPIRITUAL POWER
	SPIRITUAL REALITY
	SPIRITUAL VALUE
	SPIRITUAL BLESSING
	SPIRITUAL DISCERNMENT
	SPIRITUAL WARFARE
	SPIRITUAL ASCENDANCY
	SPIRITUAL MINDEDNESS

www.ingramcontent.com/pod-product-compliance
Lightning Source LLC
Chambersburg PA
CBHW060637030426
42337CB00018B/3395